Johannes Sachslehner

VIENNA

THE MAGIC OF AN IMPERIAL CITY

With 150 colour photographs
by Toni Anzenberger

Pichler Verlag

A PLACE OF WISTFUL DREAMS

Once you have wandered across the peacefully quiet Heldenplatz in the late evening rays of the sun, welcomed by the illusive shapes of the grand buildings along the Ringstrasse, once you have walked the brightly glittering gravel paths of Schönbrunn, your eyes feasting on the majestic façades of the imperial palace spanned by an arch of azure-blue sky, you will forever remember the incomparable flair emanating from this city. Vienna, this ancient and magnificent fairy city at the Danube, once the residence and powerhouse of the Habsburg emperors, unfolds a grandiose spectacle to its visitors. It invites us to take a unique trip down the eternal magical kingdom of the past, reminds us of worlds long sunk into oblivion, tells us of wonderful stories and legends. Vienna can overwhelm visitors once they are ready and willing to open their senses and become receptive to the serene poetry, the golden sheen of melancholy enveloping its buildings and squares. Set at the intersection of occident and orient, built into a citadel bristling with fortifications, the Habsburg dynasty's *New Troy,* Vienna has become a monumental archive of western history and culture, its fate ineffaceably engraved in stone and marble, its monuments and treasures stirring the minds of its guests. Because it unlocks memories, Vienna moves us more intensely, more insistently than almost any other European capital. The imperial town fascinates because it touches upon dreams and longings, rouses positive emotions and moods, and, not least, holds out hopes of a future urban landscape that offers the safety of home and happiness in an urban labyrinth.

Sited at the northernmost foothills of the Alps, embedded into gentle hills and terraces at the banks of the river Danube, Vienna has offered a space for humans to live in for two millennia. From modest Vindobona, an ordinary camp of Roman legionaries built shortly after the birth of Christ to protect Rome against the "barbarians" from the north and almost forgotten in

later days, a flourishing medieval town arose, first mentioned as *Wenia* in 881, to become the ambitious capital of the Babenbergs' "empire in the east" and brilliant centre of the Habsburgs' Holy Roman Empire. Vienna can point at impressive achievements of importance to global history: the glorious defence against the Ottomans in 1529 and 1683, resistance to the Nazi terror regime and the reconstruction of the ruined town after 1945. The Viennese have both feet firmly in the present but they never forget their past: it is present in many shapes and forms, but never dominant. The past does not rule the Viennese: they do not live in but rather with the past, they are proud of the past, treasure and appreciate it as an ancient mirror of their own existence and never-failing wellspring of inspiration and strength.

Situated at the periphery of the German-speaking countries, Vienna has always accepted immigrants into its cosmopolitan, Central European fold that has been open to all comers. For many of those, Vienna became a new home, harvesting their hard work and great achievements that contributed to the fame and glory of the city. They came from all provinces of the great Habsburg empire and from all parts of Europe, attracted by the glamour of the imperial capital. Artists and peasants, shepherds and labourers, the rich and the poor, servants from Bohemia as much as noblemen from Spain, Jewish pedlars and Italian architects, Greek merchants and Armenian coffeehouse owners, the learned and the clergymen, adventurers and soldiers of fortune from all over Europe, seeking glory and honour in the employment of the Habsburg emperors. The magnificent imperial town was their own great attainment. Vienna has always been drawing its strength from its internationality, its countless ties to peoples and nations. The great culture that now captivates and enthrals visitors the world over springs from this open attitude towards things foreign which enabled integration without the denigrating pressure to abandon the immigrants' own culture. Even though conflict crops up here and there, today Vienna is a cosmopolitan and multicultural metropolis, pervaded by the remarkable ability to create a sufficiency of integration in situations where racial, ethnic or religious barriers might be expected. For this reason, Vienna has retained its "human" touch.

"You can recognise cities by their pace, just as you do people," wrote Robert Musil in his unfinished novel "The Man Without Properties". The way "movement vibrates in the streets" bestows a special quality to the imperial capital and residential town of Vienna. Musil's diagnosis, applied to Vienna as it was in 1913, one year before the Great War, is still true.

Vienna has preserved its special rhythm, its inimitable atmosphere and spirit, even though it has progressed into modernity and developed into a dynamic urbanity full of pulsating, vibrant life: hovering above the hectic day-to-day affairs, the "genuine Viennese" have kept a sort of fatalistic *gemütlichkeit,* a propensity for casualness and jocosity, occasionally punctured by melancholy and gloom. A certain *laissez-faire* disposition rules the Viennese way of life and art, pervaded by a slight yearning for death: the magic of life and the thought of our own ephemeral existence mingle, to create a special effect. The places celebrating life in words and music stand side-by-side with the dark museums of death: catacombs, vaults, cemeteries are all-present in Vienna, like hardly anywhere else. The certainty of death is part and parcel of the world in Vienna, counterpointing its ebullient love of life.

The cliché of Vienna and the Viennese is universally known: bon vivants blissfully swaying to the beguiling waltzes of the Strauss brothers, wine tavern guests warbling plaintive songs, the nostalgia of Burgtheater and coffeehouses, Viennese choir boys and fiacre coachmen, St. Stephen's Cathedral and the Giant Ferris Wheel – all, as a traveller reported, "caught up in a dizzy whirligig and merry hubbub". Images of Vienna that are dearly beloved by us, and yet it would be a great pity not to dig under the surface: Vienna, this old urban fairy on the great river, has infinitely more to offer. Vienna's cityscape has remained a special place: a place where the myths of the past remain alive in every nook and cranny, where innumerable grandiose treasures of art and culture await our pleasure, a city where east and west meet peacefully and that we are reluctant to leave, where something of an ancient vision of humanity is kept alive: the dream of Arcadia and Paradise that we are allowed to dream a little longer.

Page 4: The enchanted world of Schönbrunn Park: the Gloriette, built by Maria Theresia as a memorial to the dead soldiers of her imperial army.

Page 6 from top left to bottom right: Music, vivacity and entertainment everywhere: the Opera Ball, the Mozart Monument at the Burggarten, waltzing king Johann Strauss at the Stadtpark and the Vienna Boys Choir.

Page 8: The Secession, lustrous symbol of Viennese art embarking on the future in the fin de siècle, 1897/98.

IN THE HEART OF THE TOWN

Walking through the Inner City of Vienna with our hearts open and senses all attuned, on ground where the fates of many humans have been accomplished, we feel a sense of peace and reconciliation with life. We realise that although the olden days are gone forever, we still hear them tinkling softly amidst dignified old buildings, opulent churches and imposing palaces. We float through a dreamy land of memories, along narrow lanes and across atmospheric squares, past statues and monuments, picking up a strange harmony between the far-away "world of yesterday" and the hectic life of today.

High above the colourful maze of roofs and gables, a gigantic structure rises majestically that draws all eyes and that has become the symbol of the town's character: the cathedral of St. Stephen's, steeped in legends, for centuries landmark and centrepoint of Vienna. From its lookout, the defenders of Vienna observed the Turkish enemy's advances during the second siege in 1683; and, in April 1945, soldiers of the Red Army watched the last fights with the German units. It was here that the Habsburgs staged their weddings, celebrated their victories and buried some members of their dynasty.

Within the city, which had been girded by mighty fortifications until the 19th century, wanderers are guided back into the mythic depths of time: the Roman era at Michaelerplatz and Hoher Markt, the medieval town in the Blutgasse quarter and the old "Jewish town" around the Judenplatz which today has been artfully transformed into a memorial: telling of the victims and naming names it talks of the crimes that were committed on the soil of Vienna against the Jewish people, from the "Vienna Geserah" in 1421 to the Holocaust.

The Inner City of Vienna is a landscape made of stone yet full of life, a salient space that tells of sombre tragedy and great triumph, of crime and punishment, of love and sorrow, and through all those stories has become a myth itself.

Page 10: Dreamy memories: a fiacre passing underneath the Michaelerkuppel.
Opposite page: Said to be the oldest church of Vienna: St. Ruprecht's Church, first mentioned in 1200.
Top: Monumental gate to the Hofburg complex: Michaelertor, built in 1889/93.
Above left: Stone reminiscences of the Roman legionary camp of Vindobona: remains of the floor heating system in a Roman officer's house, Hoher Markt 3.
Above right: Subterranean Vienna: medieval brickwork at the Zwölf-Apostel-Keller, Sonnenfelsgasse 3.

Left: The stone heart of the city and venerable landmark of Vienna: St. Stephen's Cathedral.

Top right: Old and new Vienna meet at the Stephansplatz: Hans Hollein's Haas House and one of the two Romanesque Heidentürme of the westwork, the oldest parts of the cathedral.

Above right: Starting point for a romantic tour of the town: fiacre stands in the shadow of the great cathedral.

Opposite page: Built to the glory of God, St. Stephen's has become a symbol of western traditions and Austrian identity.

The charm of old Vienna:
Left: Griechengasse, named after Levantine merchants who once lived here.

Opposite page, top row to bottom row: Baroque burgher houses in Kurrent-gasse.

Obizzipalais, quarter-ing the clock and watch museum of the City of Vienna since 1921.

Rendezvous place at Neuer Markt: Donner-brunnen fountain, 1739.

Griechenbeisel, Fleischmarkt 11, where the legendary Augustin is said to have sung his ballads amidst the ghastly terrors of the black death.

Picturesque Ruprechts-platz.

Late medieval flying buttresses in Blutgas-se, a lane purportedly steeped in blood.

Opposite page: Sacral centre of the Jewish Community of Vienna: the city temple in Seitenstettengasse 4, built in 1824/26 from designs by architect Josef Kornhäusel.

Top right: The Holocaust memorial at Judenplatz, by Rachel Whiteread. Monument to 65,000 Jewish victims of the Nazi regime.
Right: The monument against war and fascism at Albertina-platz, by Alfred Hrdlicka, 1988–91.

Top left: God's mighty fortress from medieval times: Minoritenkirche, today the Italian national church Maria Schnee.
Above left: "Austria's seafaring power", monumental fountain by Rudolf Weyr at Michaelerplatz.
Right: Music and melodies accompany the wanderers: street musicians at Michaelerplatz.

Opposite page: A walk through the emperor's golden city: Kohlmarkt and the imposing dome of the Michaelertor.

Left: An expanse of light harmoniously enclosed: Josefsplatz, the Austrian National Library and the equestrian statue of Emperor Joseph II.

Top: On the roof of the Austrian National Library: Atlas carrying the globe.
Above: A delightful experience not just for horse lovers: the performances of the Spanish Riding School in the Winter Riding School appeal by their sheer perfection.

Left: High Baroque splendour: the New Jesuit Church (University Church) at Dr.-Ignaz-Seipel-Platz.
Centre: Tranquil old town ensemble at Franziskanerplatz: the Franciscan Church and Monastery, and the Moses fountain by Johann Martin Fischer.
Right: Vienna is home to all major faiths: the Greek (Non-Uniate) Holy Trinity Church at Fleischmarkt, 1782/87.

Opposite page: Roots of the Babenbergs: Freyung, Scottish Church and Abbey, founded by Irish (commonly known as Scottish) Benedictine monks in c. 1155.

THE REALM OF THE DOUBLE EAGLE

The double eagle, Habsburg's legendary heraldic animal, is still omnipresent almost a century after Karl, the last emperor, renounced his throne in November 1918; copious grand buildings remind us of the more than 600 years of his dynasty's rule: Hofburg, Schloss Schönbrunn, the Hermes Villa and Church of St. Carlo Borromeo, Capuchin Crypt and, of course, the Ringstrasse with its ornate palaces and elaborate state buildings. Empress Sisi and Emperor Francis Joseph are the mystified stars of nostalgic dreams – the structures of official Vienna are still clearly dominated by the Habsburg style. Newly arrived in Vienna in the late 13th century, the ducal, royal and later imperial family with their prominent noses and distinctive lips put their unique stamp on the town: it was global politics and dynastic interests that drove the Habsburgs to transform Vienna into an occidental metropolis. Their skilful marriages and inheritance treaties linked them and their capital city to Europe. The well-known motto "Bella gerant alii, tu felix Austria nube/Manquae Mars aliis, dat tibi regna Venus" ("Let others wage war, you, happy Austria, marry, since as Mars gives realms to others, so does Venus give them to you") would prove advantageous for Vienna too. The Habsburgs were no great strategists, much less grand generals full of derring-do, and so anything too grandly martial is relegated to the background in Vienna: the canon-studded fortress walls were demolished and replaced by the splendid Ringstrasse boulevard, lined with the State Opera, Burgtheater, Museums of Art and Natural History, the Ethnology Museum at the Neue Hofburg, the Museum for Applied Art – exemplifying and mirroring the strengths of the Habsburgs: enthusiastic lovers of the theatre and music, ambitious sponsors of the sciences and arts, passionate collectors, always arch-Catholic, occasionally mystics and dreamers. They shaped their residence to their predilections, creating an immortal memorial to themselves and to the world of Old Europe.

Page 26: Dining at court: sumptuously laid table at the dining room of the Imperial Apartments; Hofburg.

Top: The crowning glory of a wonderful park: Gloriette.
Above: Tropical plants behind iron and glass: the Palm House, 1882.

Right: Imposing impression: Schönbrunn, the residential palace of the Habsburg emperors.

Schönbrunn: art and statecraft par excellence.

Opposite page:
Top: The Grand Rosa Chamber, decorated by the landscapes of Baroque painter Joseph Rosa.
Below left: Bedroom used by Empress Elisabeth and Emperor Francis Joseph.
Below right: Sombre splendour: Sisi's bedroom at the Hermes Villa in Lainzer Tiergarten.

This page:
Top: The Grand Gallery at Schönbrunn, once the venue of grand feasts.
Below left: Carriage Museum: the state carriage of Emperor Francis I.
Below right: The originator, planner and owner of Schönbrunn: Maria Theresia.

Top left: Temple to precious books: the grand hall of the Austrian National Library, built from designs by Johann Bernhard Fischer von Erlach in 1723–26.
Top right: Omnipresent symbol of the Habsburg monarchy: the double eagle hovering above the Neue Hofburg.
Above right: The insignia of the Austrian empire: orb, crown and sceptre, Secular Treasury, Hofburg.

Opposite page: Focal point of imperial glory: Heldenplatz and Neue Hofburg.

IM GESCHIRR

Left: Sisi Museum; view of the room, "Am Hof".
Top: Empress Elisabeth's living-room-cum-bedroom at her Hofburg suite (Amalienburg).

The Capuchin Crypt, burial place of the Habsburgs.
Left: Maria Theresia Crypt, the double sarcophagus holding her and her spouse, Francis I Stephen, with the plain coffin of their son Joseph II in front.
Top right: The sarcophagi of Emperor Francis Joseph I, Crown Prince Rudolf and Sisi.
Above right: Detail of the sarcophagus of Emperor Charles VI.

Top left: The Baroque world of St. Carlo Borromeo: ceiling fresco (detail) by Johann Michael Rottmayr.
Above left: Swaying horizontal lines, supported by high columns and pilasters.
Right: A monumental structure of classic beauty: St. Carlo Borromeo, built by Johann Bernhard Fischer von Erlach, 1716–39.

Left: Upper Belvedere, the summer palace of Prince Eugene of Savoy, built from designs by Johann Lukas von Hildebrandt in 1720–23.
Top right: Merry garden world: a charming lute player in the park of the Belvedere.
Above right: The ducal crown of the Savoys and the coat-of-arms of Prince Eugene, main gate.

A Baroque jewel housing the Baroque Museum. **Left:** The mirror cabinet at the Lower Belvedere, apotheosis of Prince Eugene, by Balthasar Permoser, 1721. **Below left:** Delicate wall decorations of the mirror cabinet. **Below right:** Highly expressive lead cast from the Baroque: the original figure of the Providentia Fountain on Neuer Markt, by Georg Raphael Donner, Marble Hall of the Lower Belvedere, 1737–39.

Ringstrasse: the imperial state boulevard of Vienna.

Opposite page:

Top: A house for the imperial collections: the Museum of Natural History, Burgring 7, 1872–81.

Below left: World-famous palace of music: the Vienna State Opera, 1863–69.

Below right: Parliament and Pallas Athene Fountain, 1874–83.

This page:

Top: Town Hall, built in 1873–83, an imposing backstage for the Summer Film Festival.

Below left: Lithe cathedral Gothic: the Votiv Church, 1856–79.

Centre: Intricate staircases at City Hall.

Below right: Legendary stage: the Burgtheater, 1874–88.

THE MAGIC WORLD OF CULTURE

Time stands still when the immortal melodies dreamed up by Mozart, Beethoven and Schubert ring out, and the stirring waltzes by the Strausses, Lanner and Ziehrer sweep listeners off their feet. Musicians strike up and the heavy burdens of everyday life are swept away, bubbly merriment makes our hearts quiver with pleasure. Music is still the lifeblood and mark of the imperial city, a shining jewel in the fascinating spectrum of Viennese culture: the Viennese Boys Choir, the ensemble of the Vienna State Opera and the Vienna Philharmonics tour the world with their electric message of Viennese music. Major events such as the Opera Ball, the New Year's Concert and the Vienna Festival find an enthusiastic audience year after year and counter the gloomy course of contemporary life with their irrepressible cheerfulness.

What is true for the music may be even truer for the theatre: the gusto for sparkling spectacles, the passion for playing with words, masks and roles – all this is deeply embedded in the Viennese. Numerous extempore stages and theatre companies provided entertainment and fun already in old times, and grand pageants were produced by the Habsburg court which put on sumptuous and elaborate opera and ballet performances. Special devotion was due to the city's premiere stage, the Burgtheater. Elevated to the country's "national theatre" by Emperor Joseph II in 1776, it was not just a stage for the Viennese, but "the colourful reflection in which society watched itself" (Stefan Zweig).

In science and art, architecture and literature, Vienna likewise sent off signals of immense impact: it was here that Sigmund Freud conceived of the fundamentals of psychoanalysis; that Theodor Herzl, father of Zionism, created a new perspective for his Jewish compatriots, that Gustav Klimt's decorative art and the Wiener Werkstätte achieved world fame. Highlights of Viennese modern literature such as the satires of individualist Karl Kraus, the empathic plays by Arthur Schnitzler and the libretti of his friend Hugo von Hofmannsthal for Richard Strauss have long since entered the canon of world literature.

Page 42: Vienna is one of the key centres of international concert life: a rehearsal by the Vienna Philharmonics at the Grosser Musikvereinssaal.

Top: Glamorous centre of the opera world: the Vienna State Opera.
Above: A highlight of theatric architecture: the elaborate staircase with gallery stairs and arcades.
Right: Festive climax of the Vienna carnival in a resplendent ambience: the Opera Ball, annual must-do event for the glitterati.

Top: Reminiscences of the "King of the Waltz": Johann Strauss's residence at Praterstrasse 54, exhibiting original furniture and instruments.
Above left: Franz Schubert's birthplace, Nussdorfer Strasse 54.
Above right: Music for all the senses: the virtual conductor at the Haus der Musik, Seilerstätte 30.
Opposite page: Cultural Capital Vienna: spectacular opening of the Vienna Festival at Rathausplatz.

Opposite page: One of Europe's great stages: Burgtheater, Karl-Lueger-Ring 2.

Top left: Evening view from the Burgtheater foyer across the Rathausplatz.
Above left: Lamps exuberantly decorated.
Right: The left-side staircase, crowned by Gustav Klimt's ceiling painting "At the front of the Taormina Theatre".

Opposite page:
Top left: Star attraction of the Liechtenstein Museum: room no. IX, Peter Paul Rubens, his studio and disciples.
Below left: Fresco medallions by Johann Michael Rottmayr at the Sala Terrena, Palais Liechtenstein.
Top right: Staircase of the Museum of Art History.
Below right: Popular pastime: copying Old Masters.

This page:
Left: a veritable El Dorado for art lovers: the exhibition rooms of the Museum of Art History.
Top: The monumental façade of the Museum of Natural History, designed by Gottfried Semper.

Right: Leonardo da Vinci, Albrecht Dürer, Schiele, Klimt and Kokoschka: all of them and more are housed at the Albertina at Augustinerstrasse 1. With some 70,000 drawings and more than a million prints, it is home to one of the world's biggest and most valuable graphic collections.

Top: One of the many treasures of the Albertina: "Praying Hands", a drawing by Albrecht Dürer from 1508.

Opposite page: Future-proof and spectacular: the MuseumsQuartier, one of the ten largest cultural sites in the world.
Top left: "Bulwark Against False Order": the Vienna Art House by Friedensreich Hundertwasser.
Top right: Workplace of a genius: Sigmund Freud Museum at Berggasse 19.
Above left: Masterpiece of Modernity: Gustav Klimt's "Death and Life", Leopold Museum, MuseumsQuartier.
Above right: Memories and encounters: room at the Jewish Museum, Dorotheergasse 11.

Otto Wagner and the masterpieces of Vienna's Modernity.

Opposite page:
Top: Landmark and symbol of the Jugendstil: St. Leopold's Church, Baumgartner Höhe 1, 1904–07.
Centre row, left: Artistic: elevator at the Majolikahaus, Linke Wienzeile 40.
Centre: Kolo Moser's reliefs decorating the house at Linke Wienzeile 38.
Right: Angel by Othmar Schimkowitz, guarding the Building of the Austrian Postal Savings Bank, Georg-Coch-Platz 2.
Below: Pavilion of the Metropolitan Railway, Karlsplatz, 1898/99.

This page:
Top: Revolutionary: Hundertwasser's apartment house, 1982–85.
Below left: The Old and the New in Simmering: gasometer and bizarre glass façade.
Below right: The Millennium Tower, the highest office building in Austria (202 metres).

ARCADIA AT THE DANUBE

"The city looks as enticing as pleasure," found Heinrich Laube at his first visit to Vienna in 1833, before he was appointed director of the Burgtheater. "It's good to be here, you can't but amuse yourself," enthused the young firebrand from Silesia, sharing his rapture with many like-minded guests of the city. He was perfectly right: the Viennese world of entertainment and zest for life, of enjoyment and amusement is of unique variety. It offers discovery trips to green heavens and tours of wine empires; lush leisure-grounds like the Danube Island and the Prater park beckon you towards relaxation, combined with athletic moments, a touch of countryside in an urban setting. Whether in the enchanting thicket of the Lobau riverine forest or on lonely trails in the Vienna Woods, whether walking through the spacious meadows of the Lainzer Tiergarten or gliding through the silent waterways of the Old Danube – it is a pure and undiluted pleasure to find out about all the various faces of Vienna.

Coffeehouses, little inns and wine taverns incorporate the Viennese institutions of its people's elementary relish for life. They are bewitching spots, places of encounter and intimateness. The Viennese love company, cosy get-togethers with friends and acquaintances. Listening to music, laughing and joking, they glide across the abysses of life. Of legendary fame is the multicultural Viennese cuisine, reputed among true gourmets already in the 18th century. Cooking reconciled the countries assembled in the Habsburg empire; what proved impossible in politics was an easy feat for the art of cooking: wielding Wiener Schnitzel (originally from Milan), Tafelspitz, chicken in breadcrumbs, goulash, Kaiserschmarren and apple strudl, pancakes and Gugelhupf, Vienna conquered hearts and palates, showing itself fully up to the tasks of a proper imperial residence and "capital of the positive" (Hans Weigel). Quite possibly, the Viennese may be a mite more frivolous and pleasure-seeking than other human species – but those who have discovered and fallen in love with this urban island devoted to the celebration of life will be converts forever.

Page 58: Savouring the pleasures of life in good company: a Heuriger wine tavern in Grinzing.

Top: The verdant world of wine: vineyards at the slopes of the Nussberg.

Above left: Relax and tuck in at the Hauermandl tavern in Grinzing.

Above right: A cherished tradition:
organ grinder and his mobile instrument.

Right: In the heart of the ancient wine village of Grinzing: Cobenzlstrasse, lined by wine taverns and the village church.

Heavens of *joie de vivre* in Vienna.
This page:
Top: The classic coffeehouse: Café Sperl, Gumpendorfer Strasse 11–13.
Below left: The café at the Gloriette of Schönbrunn.
Centre right: An absolute must: apple strudl with a cup of Melange (white coffee).
Below right: An elegant interieur: Café Landmann, Dr.-Karl-Lueger-Ring 4.

Opposite page:
Top left: Old Viennese Cuisine: Stadtbeisl, Naglergasse 21.
Centre left: Vienna's most famous dish: Wiener Schnitzel.
Below left: Exquisite: dinner at the Museum of Art History.
Top right: Zwölf-Apostel-Keller, Sonnenfelsgasse 4.
Centre right: Evening idyll at the Maria Treu Church, Josefstadt.
Below right: Dining with charm: at the Hotel Sacher.

Wonderful world of shopping in Vienna.

Opposite page:

Top left and centre: Unique bazaar atmosphere: Naschmarkt, wedged between the left and right sides of Wienzeile.

Centre left: Surviving on shop signs: the double eagle of the monarchy.

Top right: Bound to sell: imperial & royal nostalgia.

Centre right: Flea market: odds and ends for bargain hunters.

Bottom left: Luxurious ambience: the Ringstrassen-Galerien, Kärntner-Ring-Hof.

Bottom centre: (Window) shopping in Kärntner Strasse.

Bottom right: Stylish: the Ferstel-Passage shopping arcade at Palais Ferstel, Freyung 2.

This page: Christmas shopping on Graben: evoking memories of Old Vienna.

This page:
Old and young enjoying themselves against a spectacular backdrop: The "Vienna Ice Dream" on Rathausplatz.

Opposite page:
Top: Magic in Schönbrunn: Christmas market on the palace forecourt.
Below left and right: Fairy lights illuminating Ringstrasse: Christmas market.

Left and Top: The Giant Ferris Wheel at the Prater, inviting guests for a ride. The heart of entertainment in Vienna: Prater amusement park.
Centre: Volksgarten: a park ideal to take a short daytime rest. **Above:** And in the evening: relax and enjoy the delights of the Danube Island.

Leisure dreams:
Opposite page:
Top: Evening recreation: boating on the Old Danube.
Below left: A Viennese option: sailing in a large city.
Below right: Green paradise once reserved to the Habsburgs: Prater Hauptallee.

This page: Calm waters, enchanted shrubberies: the riverine forest of Lobau, part of the Danube forest national park.

CONTENT

Impressum

ISBN 3-85431-356-X
© 2005 by Pichler Verlag in der
Styria Pichler Verlag GmbH & Co KG, Vienna.
All rights reserved.

Pichler Verlag in the Internet: www.styriapichler.at

Photographs: Toni Anzenberger
Text: Johannes Sachslehner
Translation: Gertrude Maurer
Cover and book design: Bruno Wegscheider

Reproduction: Pixelstorm, Vienna
Printed and bound by
Druckerei Theiss GmbH, St. Stefan im Lavanttal

Printed in Austria

Picture credits:

Imagno/Austrian Archives: 52
Lois Lammerhuber (© Schloss Schönbrunn Kultur- und
Betriebsges.m.b.H.): 34/35
Archiv der Spanischen Hofreitschule: 23 (below)
The authors and publishing company wish to express their
gratitude for being granted permission to print.